IMAGES
of America

THE EARLY
OZARKS
A FAMILY'S JOURNEY

DOMINO DANZERO
(1871–1952)

This book is dedicated to Leola Danzero Maschino,
whose positive outlook and "Yes" attitude has permeated her family's philosophy.

Common sense is good to have
But never let it master you
For then it might deprive you
Of the foolish things it's fun to do.

IMAGES
of America

THE EARLY
OZARKS
A FAMILY'S JOURNEY

Karol Brown, Nancy Maschino Brown,
and Leola Maschino

ARCADIA
PUBLISHING

Published by Arcadia Publishing
Charleston, South Carolina

Library of Congress Catalog Card Number: 2005931430

For all general information contact Arcadia Publishing at:
Telephone 843-853-2070
Fax 843-853-0044
E-mail sales@arcadiapublishing.com
For customer service and orders:
Toll-Free 1-888-313-2665

Visit us on the Internet at www.arcadiapublishing.com

Cover Image: SUMMER DAYS AT LINDENLURE. South of Springfield on the Finley River, Lindenlure has always been a popular swimming and fishing place. Pictured here are the young and old men of summer in 1910, basking in the sun. From coveralls to bloomer bathing suits and bathing caps, these men savor an Ozarks scene.

CONTENTS

INTRODUCTION

The photographs included in this book are the exclusive work of one man. His philosophy and values are obvious in the humor, joy, and sense of family and friends contained within these photos.

The photographer was Domino Danzero.

Born in Italy in 1871, Domino, at the age of 19, crossed the ocean to begin a new life in a new world. Domino's clothes were cut from coarse, broad, brown cloth that would prove sturdy enough to withstand the rigors of the ocean travel. "One month," they told him, "maybe two if the seas are rough." But time wasn't of concern to this young Italian man. In his 19 years, he had already acquired most of the skills that would prove to be the foundation of his life. The greatest, perhaps, was his spirit of adventure and thirst for life.

He clutched a yellow handkerchief and began boarding the ship crammed with people of every imaginable class, standing elbow to elbow. The trunks were stacked like oversized blocks, creating a fortressed maze for frenetic passengers. The chaos and commotion seemed to excite him into nervous anticipation of this grand new adventure. Quickly, he weaved his way through the crush of passengers, securing a spot to wave goodbye to those on shore. Just then, the reverberating bellow of the ship's whistle blew, signaling their departure. He frantically skimmed his eyes over hundreds of well wishers, scouring the faces for just one. There, in the closest section of the dock, his eyes were locked in their own reflection. His father stood tall on the dock railing, straining to see his only son on that ship. Keeping one arm in the air, holding his yellow handkerchief for his son to see.

Suddenly, the ship bellowed again: three long, hard wails. And in the moment of tears, raucous cheers, and celebration, the world turned deaf to the young man's ears. His vision instantly tunneled to his father. Father and son stood silent, rigid. Their arms symbolically stretched straight to the sky. Their yellow handkerchiefs snapping in the wind. The time had come.

His new life was beginning. Domino was coming to America.

Domino Danzero's journey began in Italy and led him penniless to New York. The young immigrant then found work in the coal mines of Illinois and in the restaurants of Chicago. His travels and his work led him to the Midwest with the Frisco Railroad where, as a chef, he became the overseer in the dining rooms of the Harvey Houses and Frisco dining cars throughout the U.S.

Photography was his hobby and he was commissioned to take photographs for the Frisco Railroad. Many of his photographs were used as postcards throughout the railroad system as an advertising medium. However, the majority of his photographs were taken after his days with the railroad, and reflect the humor and the humanness of his world.

A frequent subject of his photographs was a remarkable woman in her own right, Bridget Roetto. She was the daughter of a rural family from Monett, Missouri, one of nine children. Bridget fell in love with the dashing man from Italy, ten years her senior, and her parents had grave misgivings about the suitability of this foreigner. Bridget and Domino eloped. Soon after settling in Springfield, Domino said, "If I can make money for Mr. Harvey and the railroad, I can make money for myself."

The couple started a family and a restaurant at the same time. Bridget and Domino worked side by side in the restaurant, in the ensuing bakery, and later in their macaroni factory and other related food businesses. Their two daughters, Angelina and Leola, grew up in the family businesses as well.

Fifteen years after the beginning of these businesses, Domino was diagnosed with what was considered to be a terminal disease. The couple decided to liquidate their businesses. Six months passed and Domino did not die. This misdiagnosis enabled Domino to retire at an early age with a young family, liquid finances, and an almost insatiable zest for life. He died at the age of 81 after a full life of good health.

Danzero's photographs catch the humanness of people. He had a wonderful sense of joy in life and he understood good things: food, friends, and the fun of living. He was never afraid to jump in and enjoy them. His photographs reflect the similarities of fundamental humanness and the visible differences of a way of living at the early part of the 20th century.

The images contained within speak for themselves. This book is a compilation of the photographer's lifetime love affair with the people he captured on film, and the place he chose to call home . . . the Ozarks.

One

FROM COOKING TO CAMERAS

The extraordinary and versatile life of Domino Danzero, an Italian immigrant turned Ozarker, was built around his natural curiosity, intelligent exploration, and an ability to recognize opportunities. The following quotes exemplify some of Domino's experiences on cooking and on cameras. From a 1908 newspaper article regarding Domino's cooking:

"Imagine 350 hot, juicy pies of every variety, with the exception of mud pies, and you will be afforded the pleasure of witnessing a sight which met the gaze of a few pedestrians this morning about 10:00, when a team which was drawing Domino's bakery delivery wagon ran away and overturned the wagon. The team was frightened when a trace dropped and the horses ran. The driver, Percy Rainey, remained in the vehicle until it began to sway, then jumped to the ground, escaping possible injury when the wagon turned over a second later. The running horses were checked by the driver who held onto the reins. After hitching the animals to a convenient post the wagon was righted and an effort was made to find a single pie which remained intact."

Domino was highly regarded as a photographer, as is evidenced by this July 10, 1908 management directive from the Arkansas, Oklahoma, and Western Railroad Company: "All Conductors: You will also hold train per his (Domino Danzero) request for taking views along our line."

HARVEY HOUSE LUNCHROOM IN ROGERS, ARKANSAS, 1900. Harvey Houses were designed to serve as 20-minute lunch stops for passengers on trains. Efficiency and speed was essential. For example, the cooks cracked 12 eggs into a huge iron skillet and separated them by "over easy" or "sunny side up." All of the diners could eat a hot meal and be back on board in 20 minutes.

HARVEY HOUSE DINING ROOM. Dining rooms provided a welcome break for everyone and the restaurant stayed full with travelers and townsfolk alike. In this 1901 image, the Harvey House in Rogers, Arkansas, displays starched white linen tablecloths, gleaming silver, and sparkling china. Stacks of bowls are ready to be ladled with hot steaming soup and the glasses wait for refreshing drinks.

HARVEY HOUSE BUTCHER BOYS. The kitchen crew handled every aspect of the cooking, including butchering, sawing, and de-boning. Chef/photographer Domino often captured faces and places showing humor, oddity, or the humanity of normal daily life.

THE COOKING CREW AT THE HARVEY HOUSE, MONETT, MISSOURI. A Frisco management directive from May 20, 1905, states: "Mr. Danzero is appointed Traveling Chef and Baker, effective this date. In this capacity he is authorized to go into the kitchen for the purpose of instructing your cooks and bakers. He will report to this office on the character of work done by cooks and bakers, of supplies provided and the general conduct of all matters. You will provide Mr. Danzero with hotel accommodations making no charge for same."

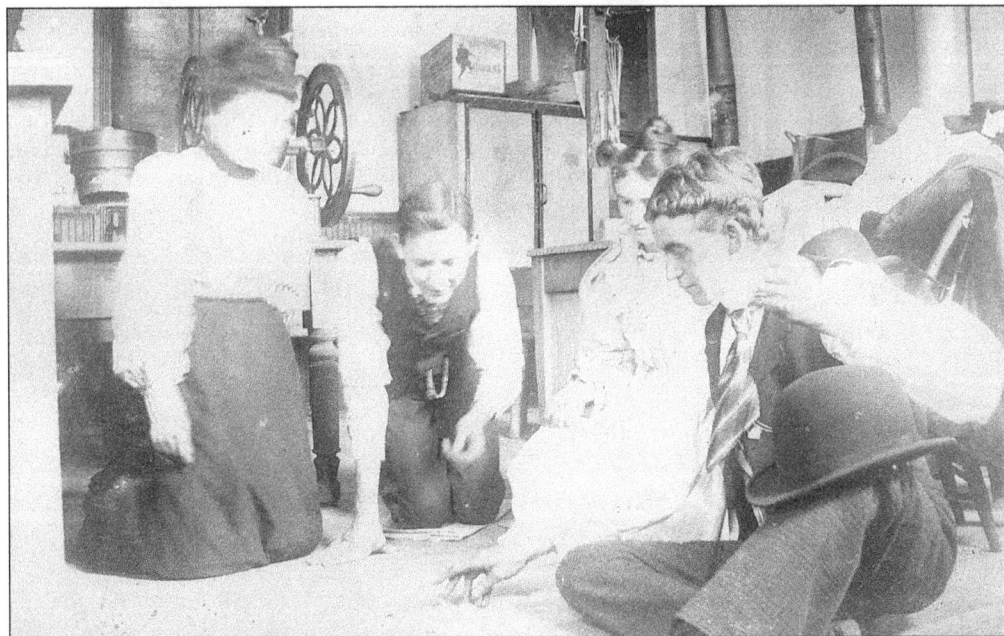

BREAK TIME IN THE KITCHEN. Between trains, there was food preparation, clean-up, restocking, and table setting, but the cook staff and Harvey Girls found time to join in the "back of the house" fun. After floors had been swept and food had been put away, there was the rattle of dice on the kitchen's clean wooden floor.

CHEF DOMINO DANZERO AND COOKING CREW. Domino Danzero (center), began his career as a 19-year-old non-English speaking Italian immigrant working as a dishwasher in a Italian restaurant in Chicago in 1890. When the wine steward came to work drunk, Domino became "Keeper of the Wine Cellar." The main chef taught Domino as much as he could, and warned him, "I will only tell you once. NOT twice." Domino learned quickly. His advice was passed on by Domino as he oversaw the food service in the Harvey Houses, the dining cars, and, later, his own restaurant.

12

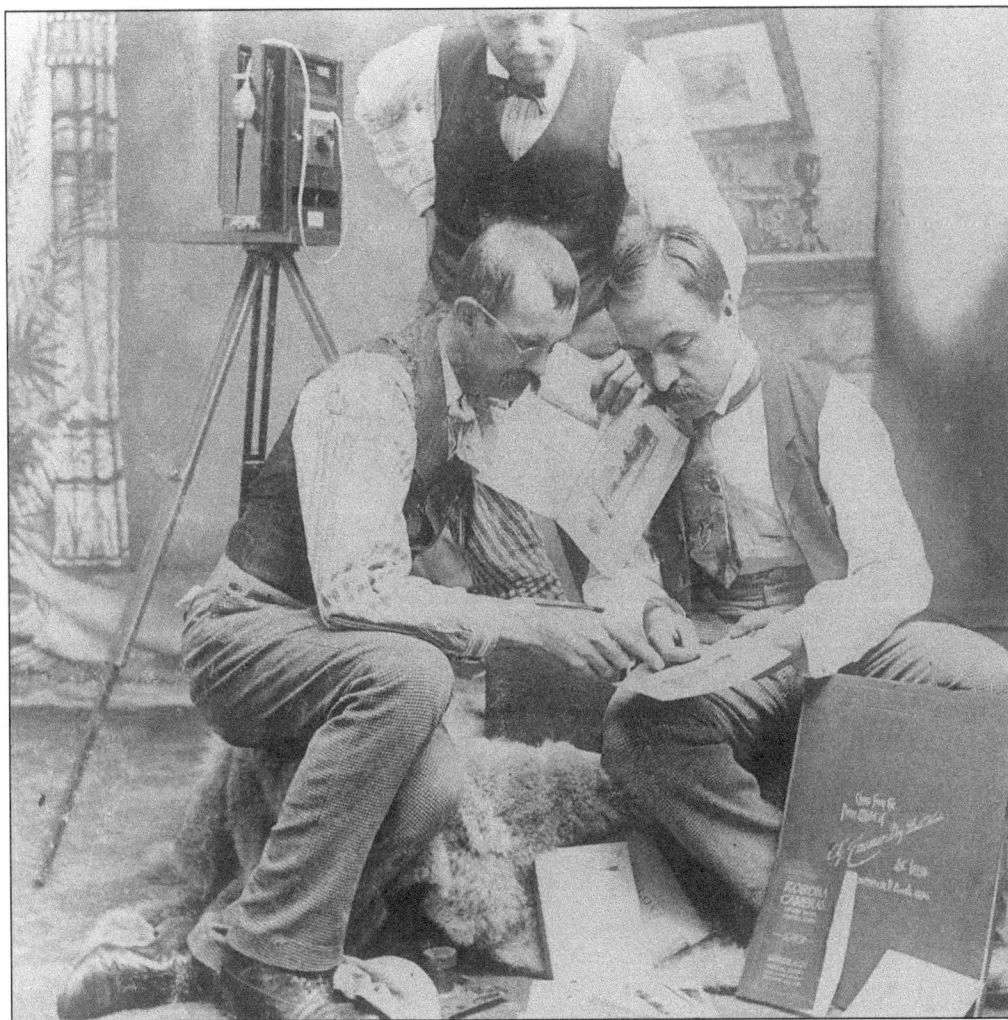

THE PHOTOGRAPHERS. The new medium of photography let every person be both the creator and subject of its images. Photography was used commercially as well as artistically, as this 1900 postcard shows. The newly acquired equipment is admired in a posed shot with Tom. P. Morgan (front, left) and Danzero (front, right).

PANORAMIC INVENTION. Domino perfected the panoramic shutter, which allowed a

Rogers, Ark., Oct.26th 1900

Multiscope and Film Company,

       Burlington,

           Wisconsin,

Gentlemen:-

       I am sending you by this mail under separate cover, a photo which I took with your Al-Vista Camera #4 B.

This is a picture of the undersigned photographing himself and then walking away with the camera, I was all alone when I took this picture, and changed the mechanism but very slightly to accomplish the result.

       I would be glad to hear what you think of it, and give you perfect liberty to publish same if you so desire.

            Yours truly,

                Domino Danzero

180 degree view to be photographed. Kodak bought this invention from him in 1901 for $200.

Al-Vista used Domino's invention, as the above ad indicates.

15

DOMINO'S CAFÉ. Opening with rave reviews in 1908, patrons of the family café could enjoy a complete chicken dinner with fried chicken, mashed potatoes and gravy, fresh vegetables, coffee, and bread and butter for 25¢. The popularity of the family-operated café and the demand for the delicious breads soon led to the opening of related food businesses.

WILD WINDOW AT DOMINO'S CAFÉ. The 1909 Thanksgiving dinner was to be prepared for Modern Woodmen of America. The west window of this restaurant at 322 South Avenue in Springfield displayed the soon to be cooked turkeys. This sense of humor caught the attention of passersby.

PIES AND PASTRY. Domino's Bakery became synonymous with delicious homemade breads, pies, and pastry. In 1907, the pie baker, Mr. Keener, accidentally locked himself in the refrigerator while 350 pies burned in the oven. While those may have been ruined, thousands of others were consumed by Ozarkers, snapping up the gorgeous and delicious goodies. At 5¢ a pie, customers took home every variety including raisin, apple, peach, lemon cream, coconut cream, chocolate cream, and more.

DOUGHBOYS AT THE BAKERY. In 1915, during the two weeks that the pie baker was on vacation, Domino, his wife, Bridget, and their two small daughters made 300 pies each night. Making lemon pies in a copper steamer cooker was like "playing in the mud" recalls daughter Leola.

DOMINO'S DELIVERY. The following is an excerpt from the *Springfield News-Leader* newspaper regarding the early trials of horse-drawn delivery service: "Two horses pulling the bakery delivery carriage were knocked down from a live wire that fell on them while hitched to a delivery wagon. For a moment onlookers thought the animals were dead, but they later seemed to be uninjured."

BAKERY DAYS, 1916. In that year 1,140,678 loaves of bread came out of these ovens, tempting passersby with the intoxicating aromas of baking bread. The bakery used 5 tons of compressed yeast and 12,000 gallons of fresh milk in the Butter-Krust bread alone. The company slogan, "Eat Butter-Krust Bread and Be Happy," was taken up by the schoolchildren of Springfield.

HORSELESS CARRIAGE. Domino's Butter-Krust and Homemade Bread made the daily rounds even faster with this new horseless carriage. The first of the motorized delivery cars, this was an original Domino's delivery carriage; the horse was literally replaced by a motor. (Note the same vehicle on the opposite page with a horse providing power.)

BUTTER-KRUST STREET FLEET. In 1918, Springfield's flourishing economy saw the growth of many businesses. This bakery expanded to include a macaroni factory, supplying the surrounding states of Kansas, Texas, Oklahoma, and Illinois. Many orders soon came from such far away states as Alabama, Minnesota, and even Canada. The plant employed 17 people and survived the devastating effects of an influenza epidemic in late 1918. At that time, two of the key employees died.

LOAD 'EM UP . . . SHIP 'EM OUT. The macaroni factory reflected a strong growth in the Ozarks as a trade and distribution center. The factory boasted the finest pasta produced with the highest quality ingredients at the lowest prices. The macaroni, seashells, and noodles were made entirely by electrically driven machinery. Factory employees proudly load the very first shipment of Domino's Macaroni to be shipped.

DOMINO FOODS EMPLOYEE PICNIC. Swimming, good food, and family fun were enjoyed by employees and their families at a 1914 picnic at Turner's Station, east of Springfield.

20

Two

PLACES AND SPACES

Civic spaces and public places have always been a significant part of the Ozarks . . . from the rivers to the public square to the city parks. This chapter primarily highlights places and spaces in and around Springfield, Missouri, the "Queen City of the Ozarks."

Since its beginning, Springfield has been a regional hub for trade, as it was built at the crossroads of trade routes between north/south and east/west roads. These early roads of commerce expanded to include a significant railroad development.

As Springfield steadily grew, gathering spots and spaces for playing were built. The primary public space, the public square, was ringed by premier Springfield businesses in 1900. An early newspaper account conjures up the bustle of the early square: "People triple tie their teams of horses, making it impossible for their curbside rigs to get through." The public square was the showcase for circuses, parades, and public gatherings of many sorts, and became the Friday night promenade. Nearby streams, rivers, and caves were favorite sites for summer gatherings.

SUMMER DAYS AT LINDENLURE. South of Springfield on the Finley River, Lindenlure has always been a popular swimming and fishing place. Pictured here are the young and old men of summer in 1910, basking in the sun while wearing in coveralls, bloomer bathing suits, and bathing caps.

21

DAYTRIPPIN' TO FULBRIGHT STATION. Fulbright Spring was the water supply for Springfield, a burgeoning city of 15,000 people in 1923. The steam pump was fueled by coal and water was piped 10 miles away to 1,000 users. These young ladies saddled up for a day-trip horse ride to Springfield's Fulbright Pump Station. Pictured from left to right are Floralee Teagarden, Marcelin Nerud, Angelina Danzero, and an unidentified friend.

VISITING VALLEY MILLS RESERVOIR. This concrete reservoir dam was designed to create a lake large enough to supply water to the city of Springfield for two months.

FOURTH OF JULY, FASSNIGHT STYLE. Lush and lavish, with a city swimming pool, bathhouse, meandering creek, playgrounds, and picnic sites, Fassnight Park has always been one of the prime parks and gathering spots for Spingfieldians. Politicians seized the patriotic day to be seen and heard, as pictured here in 1923. Wearing straw hats and white summer dresses, people listen attentively to the orator.

DOLING DAREDEVIL. Doling Park on Springfield's north side was an ever-popular park. Trolley cars brought people from all parts of town to the "turn-around" at the entrance to Doling Park. Doling boasted sand-bottomed lakes, diving boards, a cave, and a thrilling log flume ride called "Shoot the Shoots."

REFLECTIONS AT THE SPRINGFIELD ZOO. At the turn of the 20th century, Ozarkers who turned out at the zoo could watch animals, including free mingling buffalo, goats, and deer. At that time, Springfield's Zoo, located in what is now Phelps Grove Park, boasted groups of animals lightly penned together.

RIVERDALE COWBOYS. The Riverdale farming area, south of Springfield, Missouri, provides a backdrop for this common site along the Finley River. The cowboys are herding their critters, in this case goats, along a country road. The automobile on the bridge was a portent of what was to come.

CLEAR CREEK PARK. Northwest of Springfield, Missouri, a clear, cold spring-fed pool provided summer splashing, picnic grounds, shady meadows, and a perfect setting to enjoy the Ozarks beauty. Pictured here is a Clear Creek Sunday gathering in 1923. After church, platters of golden fried chicken, homemade custard pies, and garden fresh salads would be loaded into cars for a group picnic before an afternoon of swimming.

SEQUOITA PARK. Quacking ducks and goldfish shared the pond. Sequoita Park, located south of Springfield, was full of exploratory caves and spring-fed pools, and was one of the special small parks of the Ozarks. Once a fish hatchery, the Sequoita pools provided a fun place for families to spend the day.

THE GIRLS FROM GAY PAREE. A razzle-dazzle Victorian times girlie show, "The Girls from Gay Paree," was one of the featured events when the circus came to town in the public square

THE SQUARE. Springfield's public square was the heartbeat of commerce and civic events at the turn of the 20th century. The Godfried Tower (center) and the street cars pictured here reflect the growing turn-of-the-20th-century Ozarks city. This photograph looks northeast toward

of Springfield in 1900. Trolley lines, newly installed phone and light poles, and "The Spirit of Liberty" on the Godfried Tower are examples of civic space and technology of the time.

Boonville Street, located between the Nathan Clothing Company and the National Exchange Bank Building.

SHRINER'S CELEBRATION. Few annual parades and conventions could outshine the Shriner's celebration. Pictured here in 1920, the public square hosted the Shriner's celebration in all of its pomp and glory. Any parade or festival was a welcome and celebrated event for Ozarkers to

CHRISTMAS PARADE, C. 1925. Nothing heralded in the holiday season with as much anticipation as the annual Christmas parade in Springfield. The public square was the center of action for viewing the elaborately decorated floats, toe-tapping marching bands, and smiling

congregate and celebrate together. This view looks west toward the Heer's Building into what was then College Street.

faces. Heer's Department store, Barth's Men's Wear, and Levy Wolf were some of the fine shopping establishments. The social scene for young people included going to the square on the weekends.

SHRINE MOSQUE. Built in 1923, the Shrine Mosque had the largest auditorium west of the Mississippi River. The mosque was the site for national celebrities and figureheads alike to see,

MAY DANCE. The state normal school was the site of the annual May Dance. Pictured here in 1924, these crisply attired young ladies and gentlemen, students of the state normal school, prepared to perform the May Pole Dance together. This traditional event, held under the canopy

be seen, listen, and perform. Such notables as John Phillip Sousa performed here, followed later by others, including Frank Sinatra, Glenn Miller, Elvis Presley, and Harry Truman.

of the trees on the quad, welcomed the beginning of springtime in the Ozarks. The state normal school is now Southwest Missouri State University.

IMPOSSIBLE UNDERPASS. This early 1920s flood stopped traffic, but the trains rolled on. Located just north of Commercial Street, the underpass has two openings. The large section was for buggies and cars while the smaller section was for the trolley or streetcar.

Three

FAMILY AND FRIENDS

Loved children, fine friends, extended families, and social interaction are universal elements of life. This chapter shows these bonds at the turn of the 20th century. The early clothing of the era reflects individually selected and constructed garments that fit within a tightly regimented sense of fashion. Early social clubs, friendships, and a strong family life are the ageless bonds shown in these images.

Societal conditions for proper clothing demanded handmade and elaborate gowns for infants, stiffly starched crisp dresses for young girls, and functional yet versatile styles for the women. Young boys sported woolen knickers and caps; men wore crisp linen shirts under suspenders and handmade coats.

At the beginning of the winter, children were sewn into their "union suit" underwear, only to be released from it in the spring. Assafetida bags, filled with herbs, were worn around the neck to ward off germs.

Families grew and grew up. Closely-knit friendships quickly developed through individual shared times around card tables and kitchen tables. From street games and picnics to farming the fields, children and adults worked and played together as families and friends.

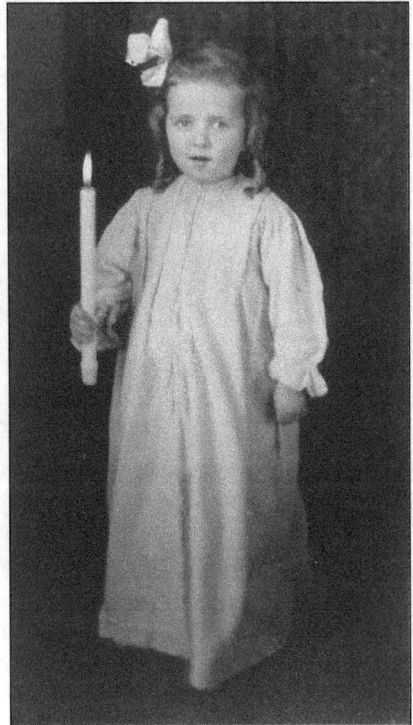

CHILD ANGEL. Children were the light of the home for most young families. With the potential difficulties childbirth could pose to both mother and child, a healthy and happy young child was a blessing for all. A single candle illuminates the way to bed for this young Ozarks child in 1907. Her nightgown shows tucks and other handmade details.

BABY IN DAILY GOWN. This proud big sister greets her new baby sister with quiet wonder. Baby carriages designed with craftsmanship and finely detailed artistry cradled babies dressed in exquisite clothing. Shown here is a ten-day-old baby girl, in her daily baby gown. These gowns were handmade with fine detailing, and carefully pressed with an iron heated on a wood stove.

STYLISH STROLLING. High fashion was common even for a casual get-together with friends. On a crisp autumn day in 1905, these stylish Ozarkers pose before a brisk walk together, having donned long skirts, high boots, elaborately ribboned hats, and even jewelry. Social occasions of all kinds were reason to put forth your best bib and tucker. Feather boas, leather gloves, and linen handkerchiefs were important parts of a proper wardrobe.

. . . AND TODAY'S NEWS. This young child is dispensing information. Posed with *Unione*, an Italian newspaper, stereopticon cards on the floor, and a series of open books, her raised hand asks for attention. She sits on a child's chair wearing battenburg lace.

ON YOUR SHOULDERS. Lawrence Roetto, the youngest of nine children of a Catholic family from Monett, Missouri, perches on his uncle's shoulders. The Frisco Railroad brought new influences, new thoughts, and new people through farming communities. This uncle, who traveled for the Frisco, was Italian; another uncle, who worked for the railroad, was German. The little tikes' older sisters married the men, and thereby brought traditions of other worlds to Monett.

ZONOPHONE TUNES. Attired in play clothes, this little girl stands high with the aid of stacked books to bring her within prime earshot of the new Zonophone in 1906. It was the latest in the reproduction of music and played the new *flat* records. Note the beautiful battenburg lace on the bottom table shelf. Battenburg lace was handmade by the ladies and was very popular as decoration.

TOY TREASURES. In 1906, this lucky little two-year-old poses with her wealth of prized toys, soon to be broken by her new baby sister. Toys of the time mimicked the household items, only in a child's size. Note the stove, piano, china tea set, cooking utensils, balls, and broom. The telephone was a relatively new invention of the time. Springfield had the first telephone exchange west of the Mississippi.

SISTERLY LOVE. These two sisters were bonded by love for life. Side by side throughout their childhood, they became the best of friends as adults. The urban girls donned beautiful white dresses (handmade by their mother), white or black patented shoes, and jewelry when dressing to go downtown, to church, or to receive visitors.

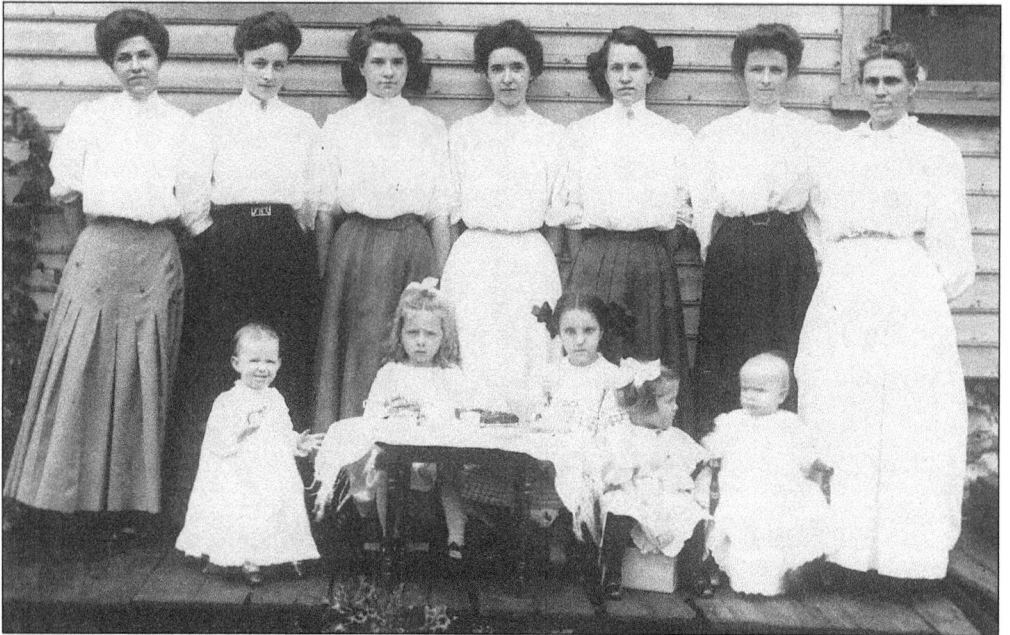

TODDLER'S TEA PARTY. The famed Harvey Girls helped the toddler's mothers serve at this 1909 tea party. The women's crisp and finished white blouses were trimmed with embroidery and pressed with irons heated on wooden stoves. The women's skirts were heavy poplin, taffeta, or serge that would hold its body. Changing the blouse changed the look of the whole outfit.

MERRY-GO-ROUND-CLUB. Social college clubs were very popular to get together for dances, parties, events, and just good fun. In Springfield, the 1926 State Teacher's College Merry-Go-Round Club members included, from left to right: (bottom row), Dorothy Elting, Aileen Carter, and Faye Shields; (top row) Virginia Appleby, Jane Temple, Catherine Jones, Eleanor Jones, Golda Jean Shields, Olive Galloway, and Leola Danzero.

SHARED TIMES AND SUCKERS. This image from Mumford Road, east of Springfield, was taken in 1923. Ozarkers friendships and fun are documented in this picture and a quote from a 1921 autograph book signed by Ralph Nibler, "Remember the night we spent my last nickel on an all day sucker and we rented it out for 2 pennies an hour? I went one cent in debt."

SOLEMN SWINGING. A warm winter day in 1925 brings a family to enjoy the outdoors. The glider swings, which have reclining seats, and an empty shade frame speaks of warm relaxing days to come. But for now, thick coats, neck wraps, and hats keep this family warm.

DOMESTIC TRANQUILLITY. Before the advent of television and the popularity of radio, family evenings at home were savored by simple pleasures . . . the crackling fire, reading the newspaper, petting the family dog, and just spending time together. Pictured here is an Ozarks couple relaxing in their home at 1055 W. Walnut, Springfield, Missouri.

Four

FUN, FOOD, AND WINE

Food and friends were a cornerstone of life in the turn-of-the-20th-century Ozarks. The hot Ozarks summers made picnics an every weekend event. Families and friends would bring picnic baskets laden with delicious platters of fried chicken, vine ripened tomatoes, garden vegetable salads, homemade bread, sweet lemonade, and fresh bakes pies to share.

Immigrant families of this area brought old customs and values of their homelands to their new lives. Remembering the lifestyle he left in Europe, one Ozarker fondly recalls, "People there do not have the same attitude about money as Americans do. All they want to do is get by and have a good time. You see shops with notices saying 'closed for the season' or 'gone to the mountains for a month.' Always they sing . . . in the evenings they cluster at the cafes and drink wine and sing until midnight. And everywhere you go they bring out a bottle of wine, bread and cheese and sausage and insist that you eat and drink with them." To the good fortune of everyone, many Ozarkers integrated these values into their new life in America.

PICNIC PLEASURES. Often the perfect opportunity for young love to grow, picnics provided Ozarkers the chance to be outdoors in great natural beauty, and steal away time together . . . out of the earshot and eyeshot of others. Seen here is a newly married couple, relaxing together in the Ozarks woods on a picnic.

GREAT GRAPE ARBOR. Urban gardeners in the Ozarks planted not only for their enjoyment of the bounty, but for the beauty their gardens provided. These ladies pick ripened grapes from their arbor, heavily laden with the sun ripened fruit. The grapes were pressed, bottled, fermented, and became homemade wine for the family.

HONEYMOON TOAST. Friends in Illinois salute the newly married bride (in the light dress at center). The bride, Bridget Roetto, went to St. Louis to elope with the handsome Domino Danzero, who was ten years her senior. Their marriage was truly a happy one and they remained in love throughout their life, partners in marriage and in business.

42

WINE CELLAR IN ROGERS. Italians in Rogers and Tontitown, Arkansas, brought their culinary customs and vintner skills to their new country. An Italian priest, Father Bandini, brought a group of Italians to this Ozarks area. Grapes planted in the hills were reminiscent of the European area these people had left.

TANTE SALUTE! During a family picnic, Italian immigrants toast to their new found life in America. This 1902 picture, taken in Rogers, Arkansas, shows a prosperous young family beginning a new life in a new country, at the start of a new century.

43

PATRIOTIC PICNIC. Turn-of-the-20th-century picnics were common place throughout the year. Although they generally consisted of homemade foods and drink, special occasions merited special drinks, such as store-bought bottled beer. Fourth of July patriots congregating and celebrating in Rogers, Arkansas.

GREENE FAMILY PICNIC. On the banks of the James River, the families of the Ozarks gathered for good times and great food. A long-standing tradition, these families brought tables, chairs, dishes, blankets, and an abundance of food to the weekly Sunday get-togethers to enjoy each other's company and friendship.

ROETTO FAMILY OUTING. Three generations of Roetto women enjoy a shared meal outdoors. Catherine Roetto (second from left) was the mother of nine children. Although she was married at 18, her father and husband left Italy to find a new home for her family in America. At the age of 21, with two small babies, Catherine sailed to join her husband in Monett, Missouri. Her father, obeying his wanderlust, son left Monett and eventually settled in South America.

SHADOW ROCK. Fishing and food was fun at this junction of Swan Creek and the White River known as Shadow Rock, near Forsyth, Missouri. Like Native Americans, Civil War renegades, and early settlers before them, the people shown here enjoyed Swan Creek very much.

SPAGHETTI COOKOUT. Early Italian Ozarkers kept their traditional foods alive even on outings and picnics. A great tub was filled with water, brought to a boil, and pasta was placed into it to be cooked. Present at this spaghetti cookout in 1920 were the Italian families of Carlo and Carmello San Paolo, Angelo Maggi, and Hattie and Paula Toronto.

FAMILY DINNER. City parks were often the site for family potluck dinners. After the cloth was spread and dishes placed, everyone partook in both the good food and company. Pictured, from left to right, are Angelina Danzero, Bridget Danzero, Mr. and Mrs. Tony Fiedler, Mary Barnes, unidentified, unidentified, Mr. And Mrs. Ralph Nibler, and an unidentified couple.

MUSIC AND WINE. A hand-crafted guitar and a hand-crafted portable wine barrel provided these men an afternoon of enjoyment and camaraderie in the early 1900s.

PICNIC AT DOLING PARK The heat and humidity of an Ozarks summer brought many folks out to seek the cool and comfort of a shady and comfortable refuge. Here, friends gather for a picnic at Springfield's Doling Park in 1908. The ladies dressed in cool white cotton dresses, while the gentlemen sported their suits and hats amid the scorching summer heat.

THE DRINKS. The *Springfield News-Leader* of October 31, 1931, reported: "Our prohibition is a joke in Europe," said one Italian Ozarker, upon returning from a recent trip to Italy, "there they have no drinking water, not even on the train. You see the passengers taking out their bottles and drinking on the train. At the stops, instead of selling popcorn and peanuts, the peddlers bring pushcarts with bottles of wine. You drink it or you don't drink."

THE DRUNKS. "And in all (in Europe) my months there I saw only one man partly drunk—and I was the cause of that," he laughed.

BAKERY EMPLOYEE PICNIC. Early businesses found ways of thanking their employees for early business growth and prosperity by such ways as including everyone in annual company picnics. Employees of Domino's Bakery enjoy an employee picnic in 1915 at Turners Station, east of Springfield in this photograph. People could take a train to Turners Station, enjoy a picnic or an outing, and then return to Springfield by train.

ROADSIDE GRILLING. Long since abandoned, this homestead cook stove left in the woods by the James River, near Springfield, became a perfect picnic site. After gathering the kindling and wood, the little stove chugged away, providing hot, delicious picnic meals for these Ozarkers.

DOLING PARK PICNIC, C. 1920S. Springfield's Doling Park was an every Sunday event for many families. Swimming and boating in the daytime was followed by the evening opening of the skating rink. The skating rink had circus type music, and rented skates stayed on many feet until the rink closed for the night.

PICNIC TIME. Men pushed their hats back, white clad young girls sipped cool lemonade, and summer sun preceded a cooling swim in the Ozarks. The three center people are Mr. Robert Knight and his daughters, Mary and Helen, in 1921 at Doling Park, Springfield, Missouri.

CRAWDADDY BOIL. Pork rinds served as bait when dangled from a line into a deep crawdad hole. After pinching onto bait, the "crawdaddies" released their grip when soaked in salted water, after which they were popped into a boiling pot to be cooked. Succulent and delicious, they were peeled, sometimes dipped in melted butter, and eaten. This finger lickin' crawdad boil took place at Turner Station, Missouri.

FOOD TO GO. Traveling with tables, chairs, dishes, and good food, picnics could occur anytime, anywhere. With the new automobiles, Ozarkers found themselves traveling country roads together, hunting new and beautiful sites for their fun filled Sundays together. Picnics, swimming, fishing, and games were an Ozarks Sunday afternoon tradition.

FAMILY REUNION. One of the most celebrated annual get-togethers, family reunions provided an opportunity to see old faces, rekindle memories, and relive the stories of the past. Every generation looked forward to the fish frys, watermelon feeds, and homemade ice cream at this 1930 Roetto family reunion in Monett, Missouri.

WINTER FOOLERY. Clowning through a light snow in 1902, these men, donning woolen coats, joke—for the weather could not stop the high humor of these Frisco employees in Rogers, Arkansas, during their free time in front of a camera.

Five

PLEASURES TO PURSUITS

The early 20th century was a transition time from the rigorous dictations of Victorian customs to the needs of new technologies. New social group games such as baseball, football, and tennis became a rage. With new-found leisure time, the great Ozarks outdoors, thick with local caves, beckoned for exploration. The longtime favorite traditions of indoor pursuits were coupled with the traditional outdoor picnic games of relay races, three-legged races, and physical competition.

New technologies fundamentally changed the way the Ozarkers, and indeed the world, lived, worked, and played. The airplane, heavily used in World War I, filled the continent with barnstormers and joy riders. The newer bicycles were manageable by both men and women; cars became a racing pastime. These new technologies, games, and social interactions demanded new approaches to movement and safety. Elaborate and cumbersome clothing gave way to new social acceptances of style. Clothes for women particularly changed, as ladies now began wearing modest pants and bloomers for biking and sports. The pleasures and pursuits of the early 20th century were indicative of the ever escalating changes that would occur in this century.

JUMP! This 1922 picnic is a wonderful example of how times were changing for young ladies. Once considered "scandalous," young women were now wearing pants on casual social outings and among friends. These exuberant young women were stump-jumping in the Ozarks woods.

ANTE UP, LADIES! Card, cards, cards! The social scene of the Ozarks included a well-loved game of cards for many get-togethers. Many games were played in rounds, with elaborate strategies, skill, and thought. Others were frivolous and fun, allowing the players plenty of time for conversation and joking. Pictured here, in 1901, are ladies from Rogers, Arkansas, enjoying an afternoon of fun.

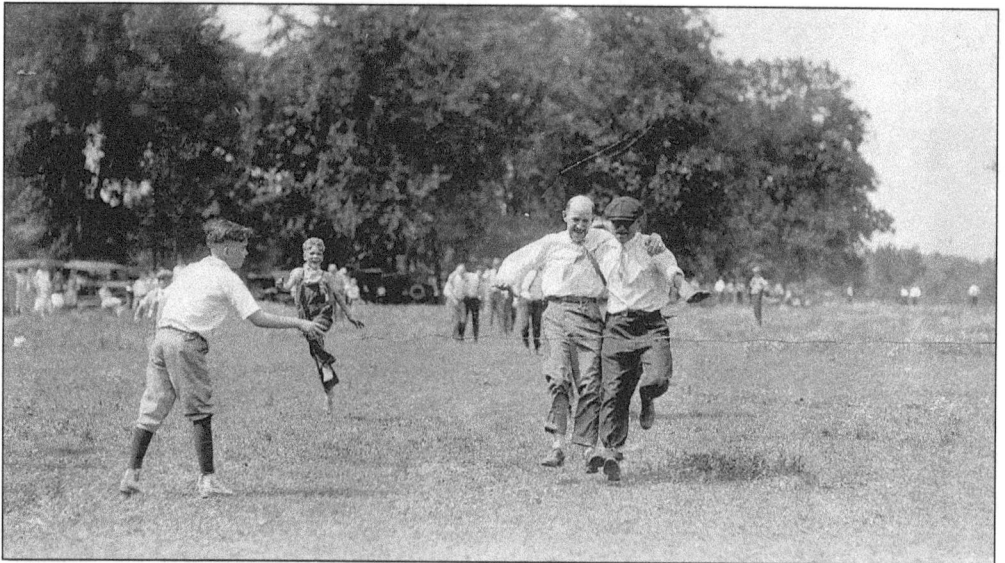

THREE-LEGGED RACE. Strong twine ties two men's legs together in this perennial favorite during a picnic in Arkansas in 1900. One child in coveralls and one in knickers cheer on the men to finish a timeless challenge.

CARD GAME. Good friends, good times, and a 1902 card game in Arkansas can be seen in the photograph above. High-necked, stiff collars suggest the formalities required by custom. Gas lights fixtures, the shiny warmth of woodwork, and the probable fragrance of a strawberry-rhubarb pie baking could complete this picture.

RELAY RACE. These ladies of the times were no strangers to good times. Family and social picnics often brought forth organized games and the relay race was a favorite. These women, dressed in their stockings and heels, managed to give each other a grand race; petticoats, pearls, and summer hats fly to the finish line.

BIKING BEAUTY. Long skirts gave way to pants for women bicyclists. Bicycles were still a rarity to small towns in the Ozarks, and when someone pedaled up with one, everyone turned out for the show. In 1902, this Arkansas woman breaks traditions with a smartly tailored outfit for biking freedom.

BOAT OF BEAUTIES. The Ozarks are home to an endless array of wonderful waterways. Crystal creeks, meandering rivers, burbling springs, and endlessly stocked ponds and lakes fill the countryside, and provide nearly year round recreation. Here, young boaters take out on the James River for a boat ride in 1917. Pictured here, from left to right, are Angelina Danzero, Charlotte Leo, Agnes Hardesty, Alden Leo, and Leola Danzero.

HONEYMOON BAND. A newlywed bride (in the white blouse) was introduced to the pleasure of music by her new husband. On a honeymoon trip to Illinois, she was taught how to play the mandolin. Just one year earlier, as the hard-working oldest daughter in a rural Ozarks family of 12, the mandolin was an instrument she had never heard of.

SADDLE UP! With the advent of the automobile, horses, once the only mode of passenger travel, became more popular for recreational travel. The famed Missouri foxtrotter, developed for sustained travel through the Ozarks' hills and valleys, was a newly developed breed of pleasure horse.

TEAMMATES. A small community in Arkansas had a love of sports and organized their own home team. Pictured here are the proud teammates of the 1902 Rogers football team. Although they played with protective leather helmets, and some wore athletic sport shirts, their footwear included anything from walking town shoes to leather work boots or patched school shoes.

TENNIS ANYONE? Women began to take an active interest in sports; tennis was one of the most popular for the ladies. This photograph was taken at the very first tennis court in Springfield, Missouri, at the home of Mr. and Mrs. Busick on East Walnut Street.

YOUNG SLUGGER. The early world series were "broadcast" by a crystal radio set to a relay person who would describe the "play by play" to a runner. The runner would, in turn, head to a parking lot and draw on a large chalkboard illustrating the plays of the game. Hundreds of folks might gather to "watch" the game played on the chalkboard.

EARLY RACING. With the automobile came a parallel competitive spirit. Early auto racing tracks required grooming and maintenance. What was the top speed of these cars? Thirty-five miles per hour was top speed for an open road car.

61

SMALLINS CAVE. Cave exploration was an intriguing past time for early Ozarkers. With underground rivers, crashing waterfalls, crystal formations, ancient stalagmites and stalactites, tunnels, bats, and reptiles; the caves of the Ozarks provided endless exploration and intrigue. The karst topography of the Ozarks created an underground wonderland.

ROPE LADDER CAVE GUIDE. Hand-crafted intricate rope ladders were devised to enable folks to descend into out of the way places within the caves. Adventuresome souls explored by crawling and climbing through precarious places to see the mysterious caverns. However, primitive candles and carbide lamps hindered extensive exploration. This rope ladder was rigged by spelunkers at Smallins Cave.

FLIGHT. Ralph Snavely, a World War I fighter pilot, became Springfield's first commercial pilot. In 1922, he had recorded over 5,000 flights and had 2,000 passengers—from infants in arms to a 103-year-old man. The Springfield Chamber of Commerce laid a chat circle to designate the "landing spot" for pilots on the field just south of Springfield's Phelp's Grove Park. Snavely soon added a fueling station on the field to fuel other planes.

AERO-ADVERTISING. Posing here is 15-year-old Angelina Danzero, on her first aerial trip with Ralph Snavely. Angelina's job for the day was to scatter paper advertisements from the low flying plane. Her flight attire included lace ruffles and a leather helmet.

CIRCUS DAY! The circus was a much heralded and greatly anticipated day. With great pomp and showmanship, every circus opened with a parade through town, with the intent to stir great excitement prior to the show. To the delight of everyone, elephants and camels marched down brick streets and over trolley tracks on their way to the big tent.

PARADE DAY! Springfield parades, mostly held through the public square, were greeted by cheering crowds and pageantry. Here, the Shriner's take Center Street to kick off their annual parade. Rain or shine, the marchers remained in formation, playing to the throngs of people who lined the streets, eager to see and hear the bands. Fancy costumed band members and elaborate floats made their way through the city streets as part of the parade.

WHITE CITY BASEBALL. Local teams grew into minor league ball teams. Semi-professional baseball was a big part of entertainment in the early 1900s. The Springfield Cardinals often played before packed crowds at the White City Stadium. This original stadium was located on Division Street between Campbell and Boonville; unfortunately it burned down. The new 1920s stadium seated 3,000 people. Bleacher seats cost 25¢ and grandstand seats cost 50¢.

MAY POLE DANCE. Well choreographed and executed, the annual May Pole dance at the State Teacher's College (now Southwest Missouri State University) was a tradition to usher in spring. Dressed all in white, these students wove in and out of each other, creating complicated ribbon patterns with brightly colored ribbons they held around the May poles as part of the dance.

BOCCI BALL BOYS. Backyard sporting games were played with a competitive edge. Keeping the tradition alive, these friends line up for a serious game of Bocci Ball. Pictured here, from left to right, are Giaccomo Danzero, Dino and John Allessi, and Domino Danzero playing in 1921 in the backyard of the Danzero home at 644 South Street in Springfield.

66

BOSTON BLOOMERS. Well ahead of the times in 1899, these talented ladies formed their own team, and aptly named themselves the "Boston Bloomers." The Bloomers hailed from the Boston Mountains in Northern Arkansas, and played a grand game, entertaining and delighting the crowds.

ROUGH RASCALS. Boys will be boys. There's nothing quite as simple as old-fashioned rough housin'. With the absence of sports equipment and the presence of excess energy, these rascals partake in a knee-jabbing, neck-locking, arm-twisting break on their farm in the Ozarks in 1902.

ROMANTIC PURSUITS. This young courting couple posed during a walk through the woods. Quiet and pensive times away from the arduous farmwork and family chores were eagerly anticipated.

Six

HUMOR AND HUMANITY

At a time when poses were rigid and portraits were postures, these images reflect the humor, humanity, and whimsy observed and captured by the photographer. Due to the newness of photographic skills and the relative primitivism of the cameras, long exposures were necessary for a well-defined photograph. These long exposures required that the subject sit or stand in a stilled position in order to have a crisp image. Due to the expertise and inventiveness of this photographer, his images are alive with fun and frivolity.

Subjects ranged from neighbors and children to strangers. This photographer's insights and humor extended beyond what was considered traditional to include cherubic infants or women in "scandalous" male attire. Lighthearted and informal, the photographs capture the warm relationships, sense of fun, and the joy in life that were a definite part of living at the turn of the 20th century. This insight into the truth of the times dispels the concept of dourness, staidness, and rigidity. In its place, we see humor, humanity, and the joy of life.

TWO FOR ONE. These two sisters hop into their Papa's coveralls for a good laugh from their friends.

OH BABY! This amusing image was made into a postcard due to its universal humorous appeal.

ROGERS, 1902. Lighthearted and informal, these Ozarkers posed for an unusually informal photograph in 1901. The little girl at the far left, with cocked hip and bent elbows, provides a sharp contrast to the stoic and dainty photos of the time.

CASANOVA. This Casanova's wandering eye was captured in the moment of his flirtations. His wife (at the far right in the front row) looks none too pleased with his actions. Also of note, the little boy's face (center) was marked from a recent bout with the chicken pox.

OZARKS FIDDLER, 1900. Playing throughout the hills and hollows of the Ozark Mountains, old-timers could crank out hundreds of fiddle tunes to the delight of everyone. Fiddles were hand carved, bows were made with horse hair, and each melody possessed a distinct resonance according to the wood and technique used for constructing the fiddle.

THREE TREED MEN. These men posed together for a photograph of friendship.

TWO TREED WOMEN. Climbing up tree trunks in suits, heels, and dresses, these stylish friends posed during a walk in the woods.

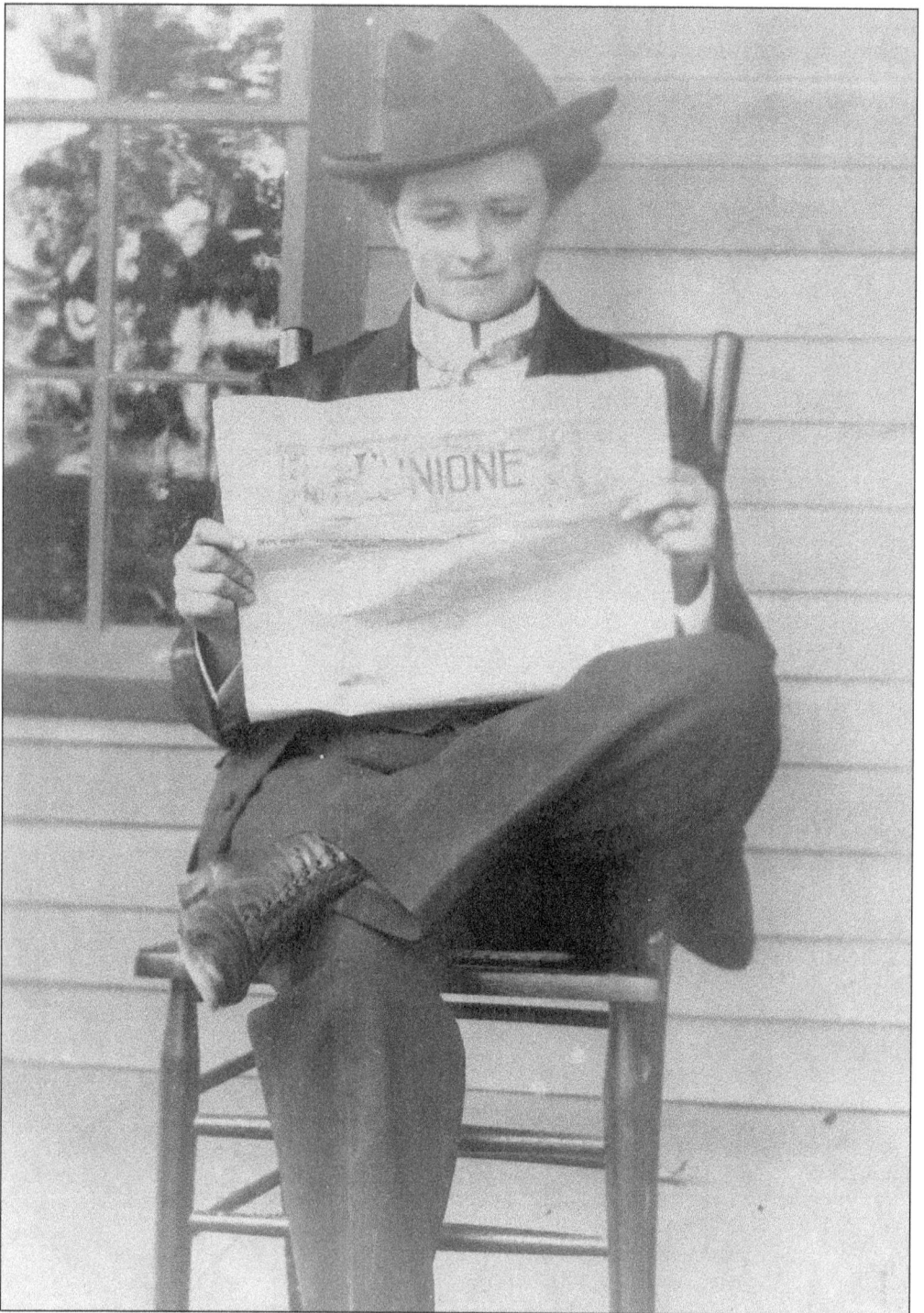

SCANDAL! This beautiful woman poses for an unusual photograph. Pretending to read an Italian newspaper, she is dressed head to toe in men's clothing . . . *scandalous!*

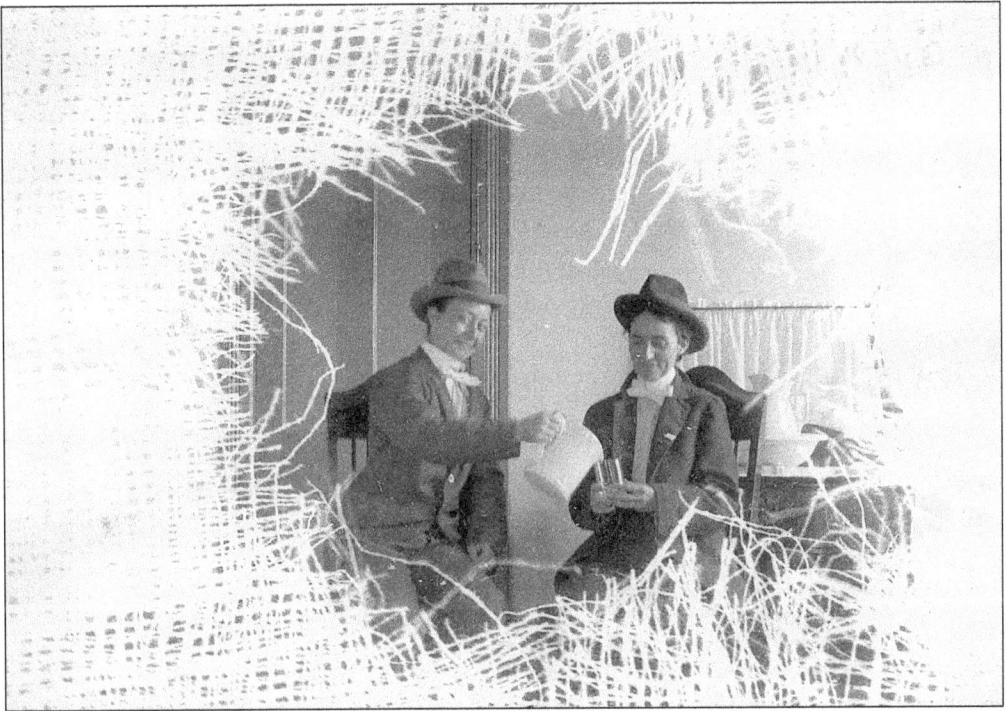

TATTERED SCREEN. Two girls in men's clothes coyly peek through a tattered screen. This was the photographer's attempt at a photographic filter.

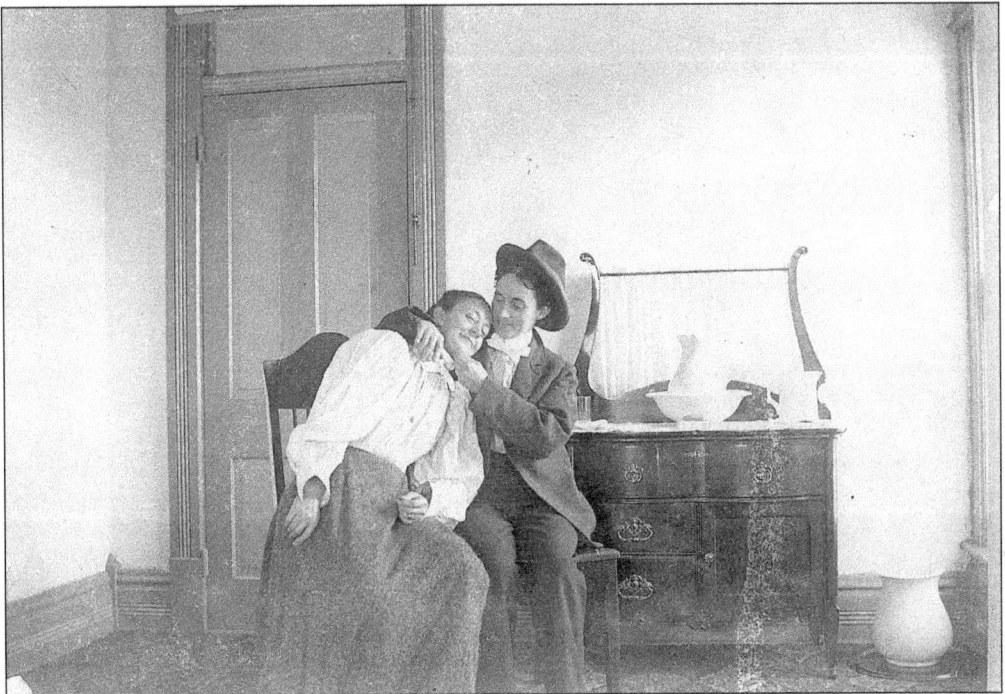

DRESSING UP . . . Dressing up and posing as men was an adventure for these two feisty young women.

HOUSE RAISING. Everyone turned out for house raisings. These eight people got together to help their friends frame a new house. With the aid of all, houses went up quickly, becoming homes for many generations of Ozark families and immigrant families alike.

GOOD FRIENDS. These two good friends of 1903 worked together on the railroad; they happily stopped to have their photograph taken. As co-workers, the man on the left was a photographer and the man on the right was a train porter. This photograph was used as a postcard.

WATERMELON FEED. The crunch of icy, sweet watermelon and smiles for all are captured in this photograph of happy days spent with the Zuchelli family at their West Elm Street home in Springfield, Missouri, in 1920.

SAC RIVER WATERMELON. Mr. Dave Leo (at center wearing a hat), with good humor and a shrug, holds up his luscious creek chilled chunk of watermelon during a 1918 family picnic on the Sac River, north of Springfield.

GOOD CONVERSATION AND GOOD PALS. These two dapper gentlemen enjoy an afternoon under the arbor in their homemade twig bench.

DIAMOND SPRINGS SHELTER, 1901. This gazebo-style cover protected the water of Diamond Spring in Arkansas. Often a sought-after stopping spot during walks in the woods, the spring water provided refreshing cold drinks to passersby.

Big Bed in the Woods. During a hike in 1905, John and Annie Leo found this cabin of sorts in the woods in northern Arkansas. The beautiful bed and other furniture were on the cabin floor. The log cabin walls, probably more valuable than the furniture, had been removed. Note the scandalous woman on the right, dressed in her husband's clothes.

Nudes. A practical joke, these photographs raised a large smile when viewed by the photographer's wife, much to the delight and mirth of photographer Domino Danzero. Great pains were taken to arrange the tiny nude dolls on river rock to emulate the poses of beautiful women, naked in the great outdoors.

LITTLE SHAVER ON A BIG STUMP. This adorable little boy was placed on the stump in the Ozarks woods for a joyous and innocent cherub-like photograph.

Seven

CARRIAGES, CARS, AND CAMPING

The Ozarks byways connecting communities by horse and buggy at the turn of the 20th century slowly became roadways for the new automobile. With the advent of the automobile, families and individuals could go farther, faster; in doing so, accommodations were necessary. Adding to their new found flexibility, a significant number of people who traveled also camped. This need was met by early campgrounds, where people would park their cars, set up camp, and share experiences. If no campground was available, travelers pitched tents along the roadside or in fields.

This was a time during which a trip to California would take at least three months, and exhilarating excitement was traveling long distances of up to 150 miles a day. Supplies were now being designed for the road. Early camping equipment included collapsible roll-up tables, canvas water bags on the front of the car, and a trunk that was literally strapped to the rear of the car. In 15 short years, transportation went from a millennia-old form of transportation—horses—to the automobile.

SUNDAY FUN. This Saturday afternoon drive followed along the White River in 1903, close to Rogers, Arkansas. Pictured here are Lucy and Riley Vandover (on the right) of Arkansas. On this drive, they witnessed some locals who came to the river with towels and soap for the Saturday night bath. Note the combination of a Missouri mule, the cowboy, and city folk.

AFTERNOON SURREY. Riley Vandover was the family "driver" for this Sunday Surry ride in the Ozarks in 1904. Rough roads and difficult terrain were ordinary things to overcome to reach cool rivers or creeks with a delicious picnic.

FARM FERRY COMING. This rural Missouri farm was only accessible by ferry. The farm was the scene of blackberry picking, popcorn evenings, and get-togethers of the city grandchildren . . . as long as the river wasn't too high.

A REGAL AFTERNOON. A January afternoon drive in this canvas-topped car with the top down was an anticipated outing for this family in 1915. The car, a Regal, is being driven by the woman. The Regal was grand; it was even equipped with a cut vase for fresh flowers.

FARM FERRY GOING.

CAR CAMPING. Camping was a new hobby. This new tent displays a steel frame that could be tarped and dropped for rain. There is a canvas floor, stools, and a roll-up table. The car was outfitted with a strap-on trunk and water bag hung to keep the water cool. This particular family camping trip was a six-month round trip from Missouri to California in 1923.

EARLY KOA CAMPGROUND. With the beginning of recreational automotive travel came the desire for suitable campgrounds. Shown here is one such campground with allotted camping spots, wide roads, and common areas for campers.

TRAVELIN' TIME. The popularity of travel added a new demands for comfortable and carefree clothing. Women in particular preferred the ease and comfort of loose fitting pants and sweaters. Smaller hats were fashioned as well to be worn in the car. Duffels filled with tents, tarps, blankets, and cooking supplies were fastened along the running board, providing ample space inside for passengers. The top speed of this trip was about 35 miles per hour.

RELAXING BY A STREAM. A small boy turns over underwater rocks, hoping to uncover a crawdad. Baskets in the cars hold crisp fried chicken, potato salad, and think slabs of tomatoes. Blankets are spread for the soon-to-be-enjoyed picnic. This 1927 photograph was taken during a typical

SAMMY LANE CAMPING. These campers could travel all day through the beautiful Ozarks and then pull right up to their handmade pavilion at Sammy Lane in Branson, Missouri, in

summer Sunday afternoon in the Ozarks at the Speranto farm near Marshfield, Missouri.

1920. Tables for cooking, and chairs and cots for rest and relaxation, made for a comfortable camping experience.

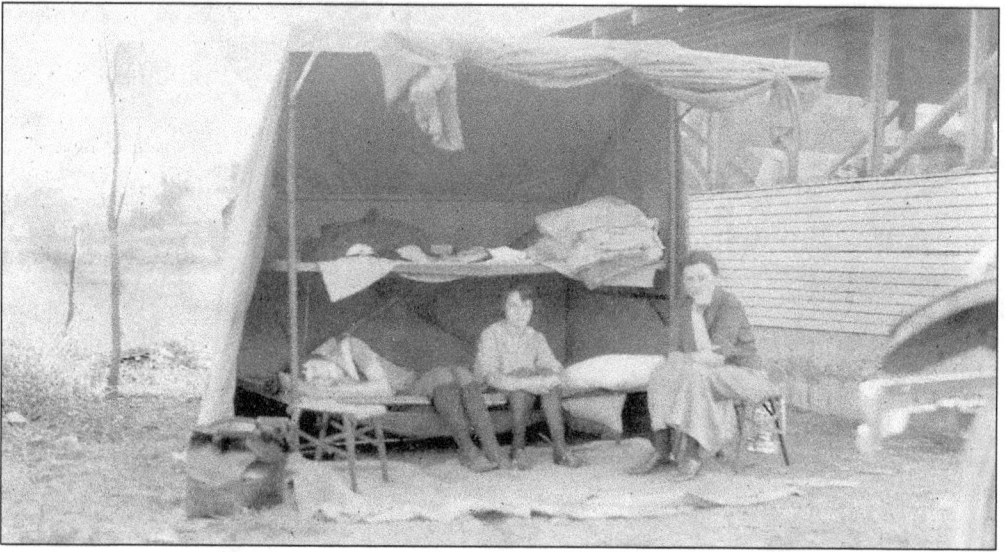

A TIRED THREESOME. Following a day of sightseeing along bumpy roads, these ladies relax and unwind. By setting a frame, unfurling a tarp, and lining bedding on cots, campers rested in comfortable style.

STOCKING UP. Small towns and cities were the stopping spots along route for many campers. Stores were well stocked with provisions campers would buy along the way including gasoline, perishable goods, and picture postcards.

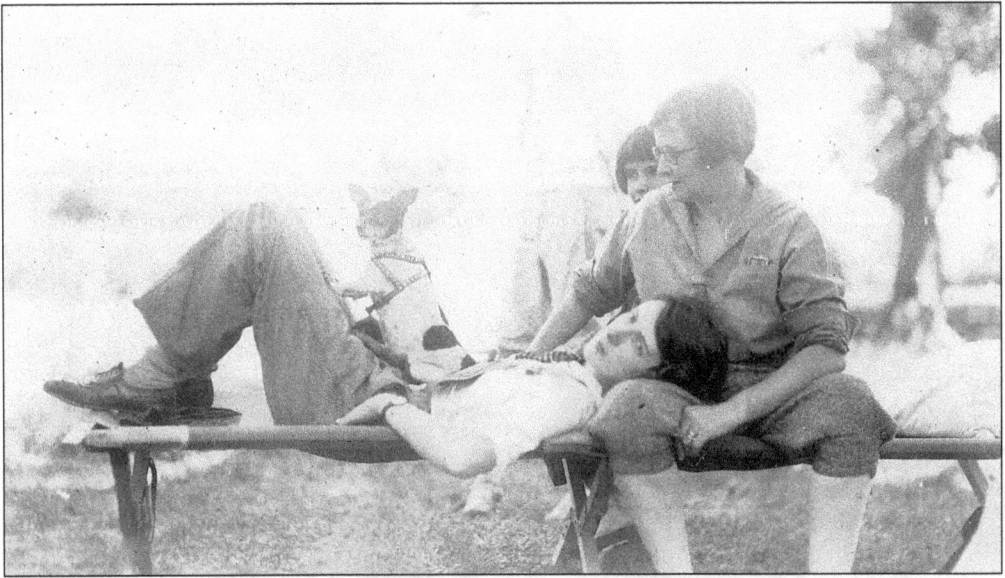

GOOD TIMES. Mother and daughter relax during a camping trip at Sammy Lane in Branson, Missouri. Quiet times for sharing are reflected in this tender 1925 picture.

THE RADIO TRIO. Making their way from coast to coast, performers would hit the road, stopping in small towns and cities along the way to perform for eager audiences. Here, two sisters pose in front of a traveling show wagon in 1923. The sisters' travel attire consists of sturdy shoes, socks, jodhpurs, sailor blouses with ties, and brimmed hats.

WRECK! Misfortune and maintenance could prove to be an overwhelming obstacle on the road. With mechanics far away and no towing service, farmers and country folks often came to the aid of those in need.

Eight

THE OZARKS OUTDOORS

Burbling springs, mysterious caves, ancient craggy bluffs, and undulating hills and hollows comprise the Ozarks outdoors. The steep Ozarks hills were carved through by water seeking sea level. These hills are interconnected with thousands of gushing, gentle crystal springs that pour out hundreds of millions of gallons of pure, cold water daily.

The earliest recorded Ozarkers were the Osage Indians. Centuries later, with few navigable streams, the isolated Ozarks still were resistant to settlement by Europeans, and initially rugged hills discouraged overland travel. Small farms ran the gamut from subsistence living to relative prosperity, and these rural residents relied on their own resources for livelihood and entertainment. The rugged land attracted a few persistent setters, whose families have shaped the Ozarks.

Rich forests provided valuable timber for an expanding national railroad system. The transition from the agrarian to more diversified trades brought the rural country folk to market. Freshly felled trees became railroad ties that brought new customs and outlooks to the Ozarks. As always, however, the rivers and streams cutting deep valleys provided fishing, swimming, and pleasure for those who call the Ozarks home.

LOW CURVE, BIG BLUFF. Ambling along the Ozarks countryside, this car curved around the sheer and craggy bluffs indigenous to the area. Rivers and creeks cut deep into the Ozarks limestone to create vistas and mountains of uncommon beauty and waterways of sparkling clarity.

DEEP INTO THE OZARKS. Cars and horses commonly used the same roads, sharing the breathtaking dramatic beauty held in the limestone bluff overhangs. Most of these early roads originated as game trails, then later became paths used by horses, buggies, and eventually, cars.

ROCKAWAY BEACH. Famed for fishing and fun, Rockaway Beach, Missouri, was a destination of its own. Here in 1930, these visitors prepare for a day of recreation. On the White River,

WINTER SEASON. The colder months reveal the stark beauty of rock strata unique to the Ozarks, and the skeletal trunks of native oak and hickory.

Rockaway Beach was a favorite place to pursue pleasures, have parties, or to be pensive. It was Missouri's first resort community and was the first west of the Mississippi.

HIGH WATER LOG. This magnificent rock formation is a landmark, jutting out of the river. Springtime brings raging floodwater streaming from acres of watershed. This particular high water mark is made evident by the jammed flood log.

OZARKS TRAVELERS. Undulating hills, lush meadows, and sweeping vistas are the reward for those folks venturing to the hilltops and peaks of the Ozarks mountains. In the 1920s, tourists were beginning to discover the beauty of the White River, the abundant fishing, and the pleasures of the warm summer months deep in the Ozarks' valleys.

WATERWAYS. Early Ozark towns often had pristine water supplies from creeks and springs. Shown here is a sample of an early log aqueduct flowing from a spring in northern Arkansas in 1901. Cold spring water cascades over limestone and through maiden-head ferns held tight to the bluffs. Watercress lines the creek.

INSPIRATION POINT. With grand vistas, treetops, and winding river paths, Inspiration Point, on the campus of the College of the Ozarks, was a destination for many.

TO PUSH OR TO PULL? On this outing, the family jokester pretends to take a swan dive off the sheer cliff of Inspiration Point.

SCHOOL OF THE OZARKS. Founded in 1906 and located near Branson, Missouri, the School of the Ozarks was the brainchild of a young evangelist. His dream became a reality. Deserving and needy students could work for their room, board, and tuition.

WHITE RIVER LOOKOUT. During a 1926 visit to College of the Ozarks, this family spends a moment soaking in the beauty and grandeur of the panorama spread before them at Inspiration Point. The untrammeled beauty of the river valley hints at a few cleared fields.

PEONY FIELDS. Sarcoxie, Missouri, was the site of these magnificent peony fields. Peonies, newly introduced to the Ozarks, brought numbers of visitors to see the opening of the fragrant

THE GREEN FAMILY TRAVELERS. Pictured here in 1922, is a family caravan outing. The Green family, an informal, casual group of many families, took off for a sightseeing trip to the Peony

heads in vibrant shades of pink, white, and red during late May. Orchards and gardens provided a staggering variety of plants and produce that thrived in the seasonal diversity of the Ozarks.

fields in Sarcoxie, Missouri. Pictured here, from left to right, are the Will Kirby family, an unidentified family, the Danzero family, the Frank Shaffer family, and the Bishop family.

BASIN PARK. Eureka Springs, Arkansas, early famed for the healing medicinal springs, was a popular destination for Ozarkers in the early 1900s. Pictured here is Basin Park, named for the curative waters that once flowed into a natural stone basin. Local Native-Americans had

ST. ELIZABETH'S CATHOLIC CHURCH. Nestled in the hillside in Eureka Springs, Arkansas, this domed Catholic church was masterfully constructed, with beautifully placed rock work, colorful stained-glass windows, and a unique bell tower entrance.

100

known of the "great healing spring" for centuries. During the Civil War, both Northerners and Southerners were treated here.

CRESCENT HOTEL. Eureka Springs, Arkansas, was home to the famous healing spas and pampered service. Built in 1886, the Crescent Hotel was one of the finest hotels in the Ozarks. It provided a sun parlor, tennis courts, poolrooms, bowling alley, a swimming pool, and horses. Each night dances were held in the Crescent Ballroom with music provided by the hotel's own orchestra.

BRANSON FLOOD OF 1927. Raging out of the riverbanks, floods have a devastating effect on

WHITE RIVER FLOOD FLOAT. As rivers began to subside following great flooding, Ozarkers took to their boats for the thrill and excitement of being in the fast moving, swollen river. Pictured here are men "putting in" for just such a float on the White River, during a flood stage.

small towns, wiping out homes, businesses, and taking lives along the way.

BRANSON TOWN FLOOD. Commercial development in the White River Valley was vulnerable to destruction and damage by the ever-present cycle of flooding. These serious floods resulted in the construction of Powersite Dam in 1912.

HOLLISTER AWASH. The tourist town served by the railroad became a port city as the White River floods in 1927. Eventually, the floods were controlled by a series of five dams on the White River.

PINNACLE ROCK. The bluffs along the White River occasionally became part of the river itself.

Sammy Lake Excursion Boat. Named for a character from the book *Shepard of the Hills*, this excursion boat took passengers from Branson up the White River in the 1920s.

No Trespassing! Although landowners often posted "no trespassing" signs, many folks just couldn't resist scrambling down and cupping their hands for a refreshing drink from one of the cool, clear Ozarks streams. Pictured here is a "trespasser" at Diamond Springs, Arkansas, in 1918.

FINLEY VALLEY AND LINDENLURE. For many years, this park and riverfront was a gathering place for picnics, family reunions, and church activities. Many brought their own bait buckets, in search of perch, bass, and crappie. A 1920s Lindenlure resident quipped, "The man hired by

ACACIA CLUB. Under the bluff of Inspiration Point at the College of the Ozarks was the Acacia Club, a fraternal social organization. In 1928, this couple poses by some of the several boats that were held for members to take out on the lake.

Campbell Soup to trap turtles for turtle soup was here. He waded our river all summer and made such a big haul that he hasn't been back since."

HA HA TONKA. Built by a Kansas City family, this magnificent 60-room mansion commanded a stellar view of the Ozark Mountains. In 1942 the mansion burned in a tragic fire, leaving the stark, devastated rock walls as a tribute to the vision of the builder. Visitors soak in the vista during a visit in 1928.

SALUTE! This couple raises imaginary glasses in a toast to the wonder, beauty, and uniqueness of the Ozark Mountains they call home.

Nine

SWIMMIN' HOLES AND FISHIN' POLES

Wide waters, crystal creeks, and running rivulets are a signature of the Ozarks. The place to be for summertime fun, the Ozarks waters became a refuge for throngs of folks peeling down to swimming suits to beat the heat of summertime.

Where there's swimmin' . . . the fishin' can't be too far away. Fishermen and women were bringing in everything from catfish to crawdads. Trout and bass, made famous in sizzling frying pans, were also a prized catch. The bountiful lakes and streams provided an endless variety of fishing challenges. Whether beside swift flowing branches or quiet, reflective ponds, fishermen patiently and cunningly cast their lines.

Fishin' tales could also grow as big as the lakes the fish were caught in. One Ozarker used to tell of a man who caught 26 bass in one cast, using only one line and one wooden minnow. All the boys shouted their disbelief. The fisherman explained, after a while, that the bass were all strung together, having been lost by another angler, and that the stringer the fish were attached to was snagged by his cast.

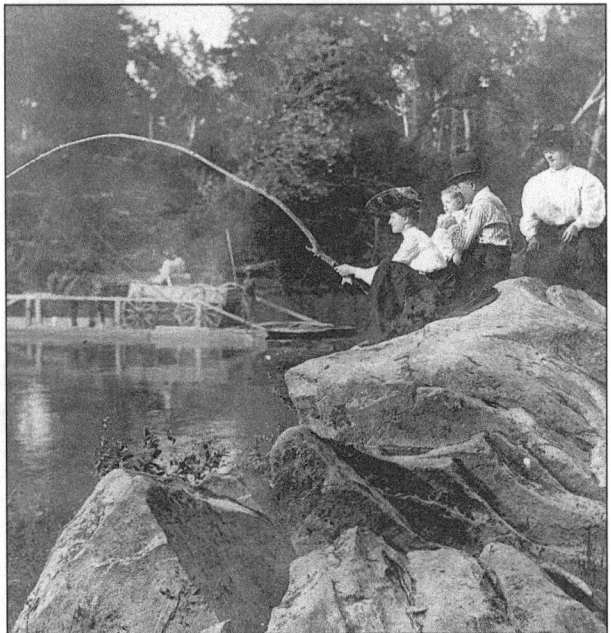

FISHERWOMAN. City girls from Arkansas tried their luck at the fishin' hole using a limb, hairpin, hook, and a worm. The clear Ozarks' waters provided ample fishing and served as the earliest highways through the isolated countryside. Made into a postcard that was used throughout the Harvey House and Frisco Railway system, this photograph showed the life and times of the White River in 1904. As shown by the background of this photograph, wagons ferried across the White River.

JOHN BOAT BOYS. Footbridges were used frequently to cross the river conveniently during high water. Holding onto a steel cable and rough planks, walking on the bridges provided a dizzy swaying sensation high over the water. The john boat and the day's catch show a typical White River scene.

CATHOLIC CATCH! A group of Catholic men from Springfield's St. Agnes Cathedral, regularly would travel to the White River in Arkansas for a day of fun and fishing, stopping along the way to pitch horse shoes in the road. The camaraderie and the catch are evident in this photograph.

"IT WAS THIIIIIIIS BIG!" This enormous catfish, on display on a Springfield street, was destined to be served at a local restaurant. It was estimated to weigh in excess of 60 pounds.

BOYS ON THE BRIDGE, GIRLS TO THE WATER. Strictly separated, the boys perch on the foot bridge cable wires while the girls cool off in the White River in their woolen bathing suits.

FRIENDS IN SUMMER. Hair tightly pressed under swim caps, these gals invited one lucky man to take a dip with them. Summertime and swimming goes hand in hand in the Ozarks.

JOHN BOAT DIVER. Delicately poised to arc off the boat with long, strong, athletic legs, this diver somersaults into a back flop, heading into the White River. The high bluff in the background suggests that this is an extremely deep swimming hole.

FISHER GIRL. Pictured here is a young Ozarks *woman* smiling proudly in front of the day's catch. Dressed in khaki colored pants and outdoor shirt, wearing high leather walking boots, she sported a very daring outfit for a young girl in 1922.

A River Run. This seemingly delicate device was actually made of steel. The pulley-style river basket was the way to a cabin across the James River in 1922. By pulling across the suspended cables, people would transport themselves across the river below.

Trot Line Treasures This fisherman proudly displays the day's catch. Trot lines are baited multiple hooks, strung along a single master line that is tied to a tree on the bank. Frequently several trot lines are set out and left for a few hours before they are checked for their catch.

115

COW FISHIN'. An Ozarks farm may yield catfish, bass, turtles, or beef.

LONG JOHN BOAT. These remarkably designed boats were crafted for fishing. Flat bottomed for swift, shallow waters, with rough cut wood and a squared bow and stern, they could be guided by one person. Cheaply made, the remarkably stable john boats would generally be abandoned at the end of the float.

WHITE RIVER SWIMMIN'. This Saturday afternoon was spent on the White River of Arkansas. The "natives" came down from the riverbank with a bar of soap for their weekly Saturday outdoor bath. The Springfieldians, clothed, stood along the riverbank to watch.

BATHING BEAUTIES. This Bathing Beauties contest was held at Doling Park around 1920. These scandalous bathing suits were a type of knit wool and showed far too much of the body. Families would take the trolley to Doling Park. In the summer, Sunday band concerts were performed by "Little Hoover and His Big Band."

BATHING BEAUTY CONTESTANT NO. 1.

BATHING BEAUTY CONTESTANT NO. 2.

TAKING THE PLUNGE. Diving into the sand-bottomed lake at Doling Park in Springfield, Missouri, was a popular pastime for swimmers of all ages.

BELLY FLOP. Divers perfected their form throughout the summer. Here, one diver makes the plunge into a tummy-smacking belly flop from the middle board while his friends watch. Boaters on Doling Lake rowed and paddled by the swimmers.

STYLING SWIMMERS. Bathing suits (on the right) consisted of several garments. First, there was the suit, with an overdress down to the knee, covering the bloomers. Second, there was the bloomers, worn to just below the knee. Third, there were stockings worn up under the bloomers. The girl on the left was daring, choosing not to wear stockings to cover her legs. Old shoes completed the swimming attire.

JUST BEING. For many families, a happy day meant lazily wading in the cool waters of the river. Crawdads, minnows, and dragonflies flit over and under the clear Ozarks streams. Just being in the Ozarks is its own pleasure.

SKINNY DIPPIN' AND RUFFLES. A vigorous group of young boys shed their clothes to enjoy the clean bracing waters on a hot summer day. Meanwhile, a demure Ozarks daughter delicately holds her ruffled skirt above the water at her ankles.

DINNER TIME. A happy fisherman smiles broadly in anticipation of dinner. His recipe? Place one heaping spoon of butter that in a skillet hot enough to make the butter sizzle; place the cleaned trout in the foaming butter; brown both sides of the fish and cook till crisp on the outside. That's trout—Ozarks style!

FINE FISHERMEN. These fellas with their full string lines pose with pride. Seen here, from left to right, are Domino Danzero, Mr. Zuchelli with his stepson, and Mr. Mazzachino. These fish might be prepared in an Italian manner of cooking, don't you think? Perhaps they would season the fish with a little lemon, garlic, anchovies, tomatoes, and wine.

TWO GIANT CATFISH! A 1926 fishing trip resulted in catching these two mammoth-sized catfish. This fisherman hefts the mighty fish for this photograph as proof of the catch.

SMOOTH WATERS. Paddling through the glassy mirrored water, these two boaters make their way through the birdcalls and bending branches of Missouri's White River.

124

WHITE RIVER DAYS. The abundance of fish brought many Ozarkers weekly to the river to cast in the hopes of a fish fry dinner. Here, Anna Minick (far right) poses with her catch of the day.

THE END.

ACKNOWLEDGMENTS

You stand at the end of the past
where the future begins.
You are the link between what has been and
what is yet to be.

My grandfather took these photographs; my grandmother kept these photographs; my mother kept the stories and the people captured in the photographs alive in her mind and heart. My daughter brought the stories and places alive with her words.

Each person, each generation, has had a vital and essential element in the framing of this book. I thank them all for the richness that they have given to my life. I hope you savor this book and reflect on your own family photographs and their stories. We can glimpse other lives and other times with family photographs.

I thank our family—Gary, Brian, Jen, and Julie—for the encouragement and support as we began this project. With a grateful heart, I wish also to acknowledge those friends who helped in the preparation of this book. Thank you to Bob Linder for his initial support and review of the photographs. Thanks to Elise Crain, Julie March, and Phyllis VanderNaaald for historical information. I owe a debt of gratitude to Chris Miller, Jane Krone Corley, TJ Droyer, and Mark Shipley for technical assistance and editorial support in this project.

—Nancy Maschino Brown

REPRINT INFORMATION

The photographs in this book may be ordered in various sizes. For information concerning sizes, prices, and finishes, please send a self addressed stamped envelope to:

Vintage Photographs by Domino
1360 E Meadowmere
Springfield, Missouri 65804

Please identify the photographs that you are particularly interested in by page number and title.

Visit us at
arcadiapublishing.com

www.ingramcontent.com/pod-product-compliance
Lightning Source LLC
Chambersburg PA
CBHW080855100426
42812CB00007B/2036